Hear Them Roar!

14 Endangered Animals from Around the World

INTRODUCTION

All around the world, animals are suited to the specific habitat in which they live. Unfortunately, some animals that once thrived are now in danger of becoming extinct.

The International Union for Conservation of Nature (IUCN) classifies animals into groups based on their risk level. This list is known as the Red List of Threatened Species. The groups are:

- **LEAST CONCERN**—The species population is widespread and plentiful.
- **NEAR THREATENED**—A species that is likely to qualify for a threatened category in the near future.
- **VULNERABLE**—A species whose population has declined by almost 50 percent.
- **ENDANGERED**—A species whose population has declined by almost 75 percent.
- **CRITICALLY ENDANGERED**—A species whose population has almost completely disappeared.
- **EXTINCT IN THE WILD**—A species that only survives in captivity, such as zoos, or well outside its natural range. This classification occurs when an animal hasn't been found in its native habitat for many years.
- **EXTINCT**—A species where there is no reasonable doubt that all remaining individuals have died.

Human activity is the primary reason for modern animal extinction. Humans cause habitat loss by clearing wilderness for buildings or for farming. We also hunt for food, for trophies, or to rid ourselves of "pests." Even animals that we keep as pets can disrupt natural habitats.

Animals that do not normally belong in an area are called *invasive species*. They are introduced when pets are lost or released into the wild. Small animals like rats can also stow away on ships and in cargo and disrupt an area's natural balance when they arrive at new ports.

Some animals are also in danger from being used in traditional medicine. This means the animals are killed because people believe that some part of that animal will improve the health of humans.

Many people—from grownups (like scientists, lawmakers, and volunteers) to kids—are working to help save these animals from extinction. They are cleaning and protecting land, breeding animals for release in the wild, stopping illegal hunters (known as poachers), and educating others about the needs and benefits of each animal.

Even small actions—such as making sure you never litter or never buy items that come from endangered animals, like ivory—can go a long way toward protecting animals.

QUICK FACTS

- The black-footed ferret is an **ENDANGERED** mammal found in mid-western North America.
- They are the only ferrets native to North America.

BLACK-FOOTED FERRET

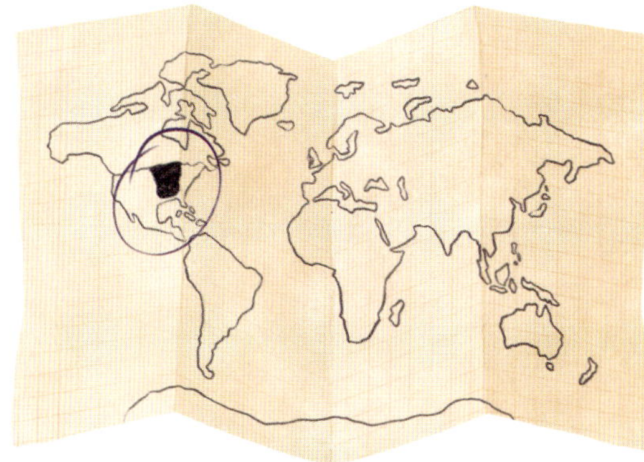

The black-footed ferret can reach twenty-four inches long but only weigh between one-and-a-half and two-and-a-half pounds. Females are called jills, and males are called hobs. They are nocturnal, meaning they are most active at night. They have great vision, hearing, and sense of smell, which helps them hunt at night and in dark tunnels.

Slinky bodies help the black-footed ferret dart into tunnels while hunting prairie dogs—which make up 90 percent of their diet—and later take over their abandoned tunnels. A healthy black-footed ferret needs to eat one prairie dog every three to four days. They will also eat mice, rats, birds, and rabbits.

The black-footed ferret lives most of its life alone, except during mating season or while the female is raising her young. The female typically has a litter of about three babies, known as kits, but litters as large as ten kits have been recorded! The babies are completely helpless at birth and their eyes do not open until they are about one month old. Once they are old enough, the mother will take them hunting at night.

ANIMAL VOICE

Black-footed ferrets make several sounds. Males make a chortling sound to call to their mates, and females make a whimpering sound when calling their young. These ferrets will hiss when aggressive or scared. Their frequent chatter is their most common sound and is used as an alarm call.

WHAT ARE WE DOING?

Once thought to be extinct, a small group of black-footed ferrets was discovered in 1981. Those eighteen individuals were captured and put into a breeding program. The US Fish and Wildlife Service, along with a select group of zoos, has helped use these programs to bring the black-footed ferret back from the edge of extinction. Maintaining healthy habitats and a healthy prairie dog population is also important to the black-footed ferrets' survival.

QUICK FACTS

- The Sumatran orangutan is a **CRITICALLY ENDANGERED** primate found in the forests of the Indonesian island of Sumatra.
- Several types of trees rely on the Sumatran orangutan to distribute their seeds. Without the orangutans, those trees could disappear.

SUMATRAN ORANGUTAN

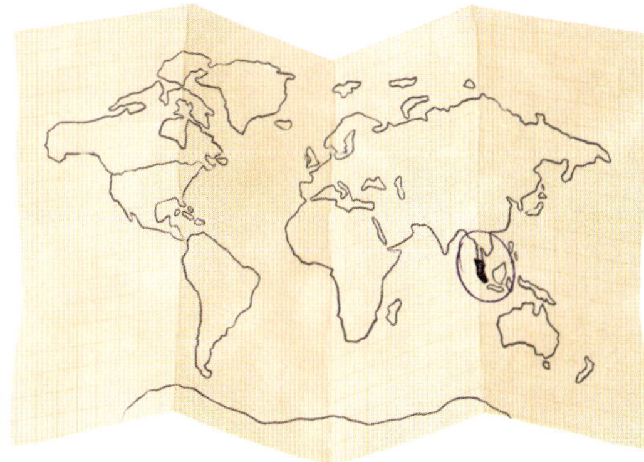

The name *orangutan* means *person of the forest*, which is fitting because these primates are one of the closest genetic relatives to humans. Like humans, they are smart. For instance, they teach and learn from each other. They also use tools: sticks are used for getting bugs out of holes, and leaves are used as gloves for handling prickly fruit.

Spending most of their lives in the trees, orangutans search for fruit, which makes up most of their diet. Their feet are similar to hands, allowing them to use both hands and feet to climb, eat, and use tools. Their arms are one-and-a-half times longer than their legs and help them climb and swing with ease. Each evening, they build a new nest of branches and leaves in the trees to sleep safely for the night. Some even make pillows to sleep on!

Female Sumatran orangutans only have babies every eight or nine years. Each baby is carried on their mother's back for about two years, and continues to nurse for another three or four years after that. Once they are grown, the young go off on their own.

Orangutans can live thirty-five to forty-five years in the wild and up to fifty years under human care.

ANIMAL VOICE

Sumatran orangutans make many different sounds, including kiss-squeaks, long calls, barks, and hoots. The males have large throat sacs that amplify their long calls. They use these long calls to attract females and claim their territory.

WHAT ARE WE DOING?

Conservationists are rescuing orangutans that have been illegally kept as pets, as well as orangutan orphans, and teaching them how to survive in the wild. They must teach them everything, including how to climb trees, find food, and build nests.

Palm oil plantations and other human developments have destroyed the orangutans' habitat. Conservation groups and multiple governments are working together to protect natural areas. Conservation groups are also teaching people at palm oil plantations how to reduce human-orangutan conflict.

QUICK FACTS

- The kākāpō is a **CRITICALLY ENDANGERED** bird found in the forests of New Zealand.
- This large bird may have wings, but the kākāpō is the world's only flightless parrot.

KĀKĀPŌ

The kākāpō is a strange bird. Known as the owl parrot, this large, nocturnal fowl waddles, climbs, and coasts through the forests of New Zealand. It smells sweet, like honey. The females can grow to be about three pounds, and the males almost five pounds. The kākāpō is one of the longest-living birds on the planet. Their lifespan is about sixty years, but one kākāpō was recorded to be ninety years old!

Kākāpōs will only breed during years when fruit is plentiful. This means that they only have babies every two to four years when certain trees bear fruit. Females lay one to four eggs and are the only ones who care for the chicks.

At one time, these birds had a huge population with only eagles as predators. Their numbers rapidly declined when European settlers brought in invasive species—like dogs, cats, and stoats—that prey on the kākāpō.

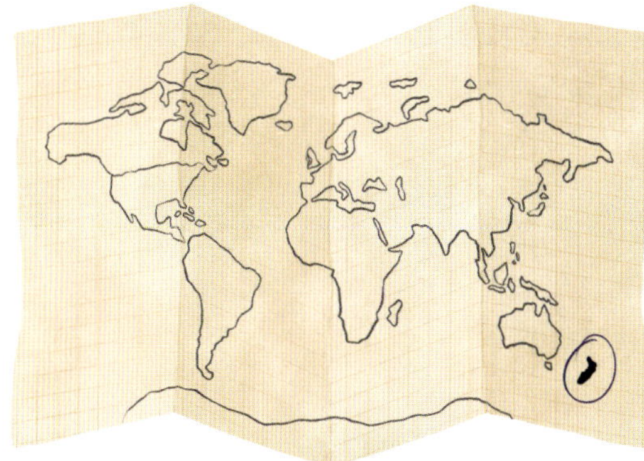

ANIMAL VOICE

The kākāpō has several different vocalizations. When males are looking to attract a mate, they dig bowl-like holes in the earth. Sitting in their bowl, they alternate between booming and chinging sounds. These attention grabbing "booms" can happen every few seconds and can be heard up to three miles away! They then make a "ching" sound so the females can pinpoint their location. These calls can last for hours every night for months at a time.

WHAT ARE WE DOING?

Scientists, rangers, and volunteers work to help these birds thrive in many ways. The most important is filling feeding stations because the kākāpōs need plenty of food to be healthy enough to breed. These people also help control the predator population around the island.

Chicks that the mother cannot care for are hand-raised. These hand-raised chicks are returned to the wild at about four months old. In 2019, for the first time in seventy years, the wild kākāpō population reached over two hundred birds!

QUICK FACTS

- The polar bear is a **VULNERABLE** mammal found in the oceans and on the ice in the Arctic.
- Their fur is not white! Polar bear fur is hollow and see-through. When light hits it, it looks white. The skin underneath is actually black.

POLAR BEAR

Polar bears are the largest land-based predator on Earth, weighing up to 1,700 pounds. Their main food is seal. They wait patiently at the holes in the ice where the seals come up for air, then dart forward. Their long necks and claws (which can be two inches long) help them catch their prey in those small holes.

Their bodies help them in the water too. Large front paws work as paddles, and a thick layer of fat keeps them warm and helps them float. Their long necks help keep their heads above the water.

Mothers give birth to one or two cubs, occasionally even three. They are raised in a den for three or four months before venturing out into the cold. The cubs will stay with their mother for two to three years before they go off on their own.

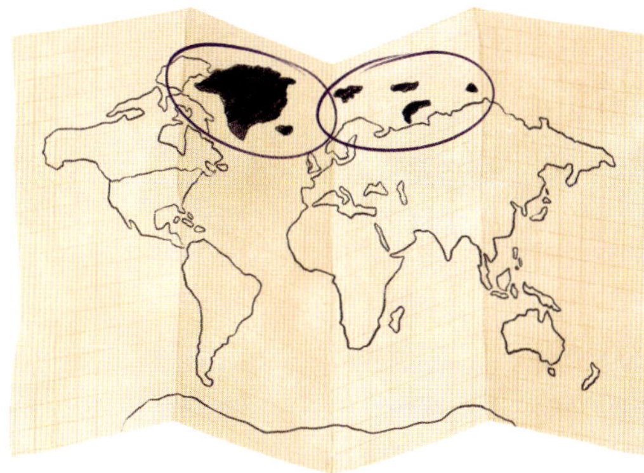

ANIMAL VOICE

These quiet hunters are not very vocal, but they do roar, rumble, and chuff. They may give warnings to others or call to attract a mate. Cubs hum to their mothers.

WHAT ARE WE DOING?

Polar bears use the ice for hunting and to create dens to help raise their young. Loss of sea ice due to rising global temperatures means that polar bears must swim much farther in order to find food or mates. Humans must reduce greenhouse gas emissions to stop global warming and protect the polar bears' habitat.

QUICK FACTS

- The cotton-top tamarin is a **CRITICALLY ENDANGERED** primate only found in a small, forested area of northwestern Colombia.
- Most pregnancies result in non-identical twins.

COTTON-TOP TAMARIN

Named for the distinctive white crest around its head, the cotton-top tamarin is one of the most endangered primates in the world. Weighing less than one pound, they are about eight to ten inches long, not including their tails, which themselves can be ten to sixteen inches long! Claw-like nails help them move through the forest treetops.

They have a lifespan of about thirteen years in the wild, though the oldest known cotton-top tamarin lived to age twenty-four!

Cotton-top tamarins live in closely bonded groups of two to seven individuals. Social grooming is one way they build bonds, and it helps keep the animals healthy by removing bugs. Living in the trees, their diet consists of fruit, sap, insects, and small animals.

Typically only the dominant female breeds, likely giving birth to twins. The group alloparents, which means that even members that are not the biological parents will help care for the infants. Males or older siblings will carry the young and give them back to the mother so she can feed them. At about four weeks old, the young start on soft foods in addition to milk.

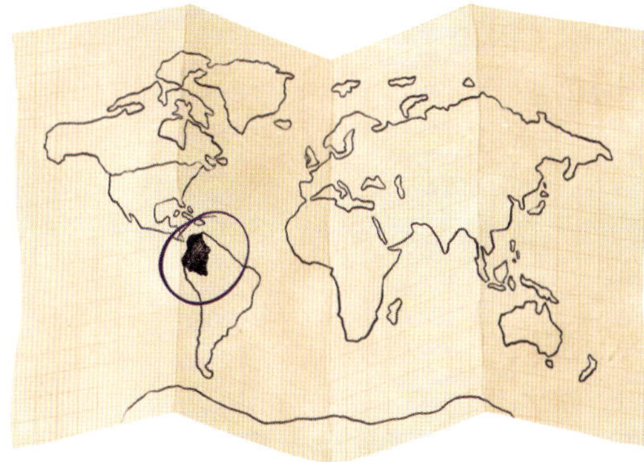

ANIMAL VOICE

The main vocalizations of the cotton-top tamarin are whistles and chirps. Researchers have identified thirty-eight different vocalizations! They also use body language and scent to communicate with their fellow primates. When showing aggression, they raise the white crest on their heads to appear larger.

WHAT ARE WE DOING?

In the 1960s and 1970s, thousands of cotton-top tamarins were sent to the United States for medical research. Now, deforestation—due to mining, agriculture, construction, and illegal logging—is the biggest threat to the cotton-top tamarin. They are also collected for the illegal pet trade.

Conservation groups educate people and work with zoos for support. Breeding programs rebuild the population. Conservation groups, researchers, and scientists use satellite imagery to identify forests that are best-suited for the cotton-top tamarins. They are also building links between small forests by planting trees so the cotton-top tamarin can move through uninterrupted forest.

QUICK FACTS

- The red wolf is a **CRITICALLY ENDANGERED** mammal found in eastern North Carolina.
- Red wolves were declared *Extinct in the Wild* in 1980. They were bred in captivity and, in 1987, were reintroduced to the wild in hopes of rebuilding the wild population.

RED WOLF

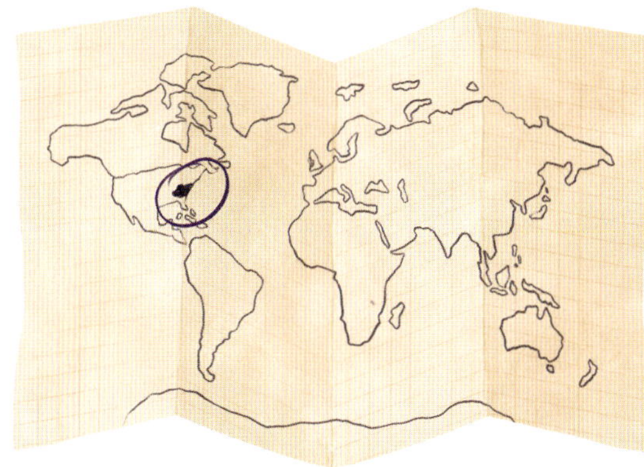

Named for the reddish tint to their fur, these wolves grow to about twenty-six inches tall and weigh between forty-five and eighty pounds. They live and hunt in family units known as packs. Packs usually have five to eight wolves. Red wolves mate for life.

The pack is important for the wolves. By working together, wolves take down large prey like deer, take turns watching over and feeding the cubs so the parents can hunt, and protect each other and their territory.

Red wolves are carnivores that eat deer or small animals, like rabbits. They can eat five pounds of food per day, but sometimes go days without a meal.

Once spanning from southern Texas up to southern New York, the red wolf is now only found in eastern North Carolina. Their population was destroyed by humans when predator-control programs were put in place to protect livestock. Red wolves also lost their habitat when people developed the land.

ANIMAL VOICE

Red wolves are known for their howling, but they also bark, growl, and whine. Communication is an important part of their pack structure; they howl to claim their territory, warn others away, and call to pack members. Body language is also important for communication. They bow to show playfulness, bare their teeth to show aggression, and crouch low and tuck their tails to show fear or submission.

WHAT ARE WE DOING?

Conservation groups have been working to rebuild the red wolf population since 1987, when they first released captive-bred red wolves into the wild. With less than fifty red wolves alive in the wild as of 2020, there's still a long way to go. Conservationists work toward saving them by protecting their habitat, captive breeding and releasing, and creating laws to protect them from hunters and poachers.

QUICK FACTS

- The Asian elephant is an **ENDANGERED** mammal found in the forests and grasslands of Asia.
- Asian elephants can swim and run up to fifteen miles per hour, but they cannot jump.

ASIAN ELEPHANT

The largest land mammal in Asia, the Asian elephant can grow to nearly ten feet tall and weigh up to eleven thousand pounds! They live in family units led by a female called the matriarch. She is usually the oldest, and she leads her family in finding food and water, as well as avoiding danger.

These elephants roam through dense forests, creating pathways for other animals. A single adult elephant can eat up to three hundred pounds of food each day! The grasses, roots, fruit, and bark they eat are not fully digested; as a result, their dung helps spread and fertilize seeds. This means they are very important to the growth of the forests they live in.

Although powerful, an elephant's trunk is gentle enough to pick up a coin from a flat surface. Elephants sometimes use tools, such as a long branch, for scratching places their trunks or tails cannot reach.

Not all Asian elephants have tusks, which are basically long teeth. Mostly the males have them—although some do not—but the few females that do have them have smaller tusks than the males. They use their tusks to peel bark, lift objects, dig for water, and protect their trunks.

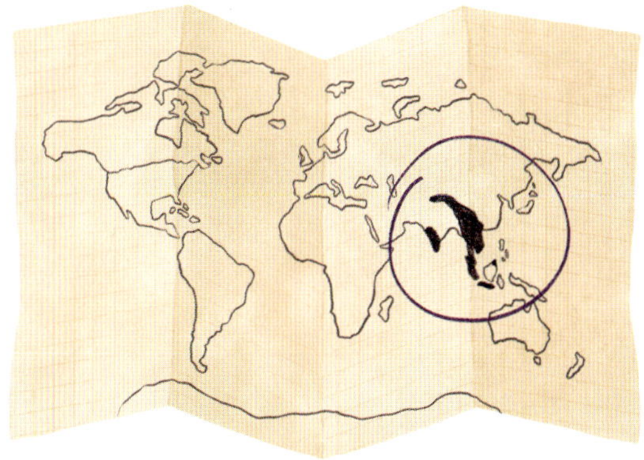

ANIMAL VOICE

Elephants make several sounds. They trumpet, rumble, snort, roar, bark, and cry. Some of their sounds are so low, humans cannot hear them. Touch is also an important way that elephants communicate with each other.

WHAT ARE WE DOING?

Elephants are hunted for their ivory tusks. They are also captured in the wild for use in tourist attractions. "Breaking" an elephant, or making it behave on command, is often cruel and involves using fear to make it obey.

Patrol units catch poachers, which helps save elephant lives. Conservation groups work with locals to find ways to reduce human-elephant conflict (such as elephants eating farmers' crops), educate tourists so they do not support businesses that harm these endangered animals, and protect and restore the elephant's habitat.

QUICK FACTS

- The Houston toad is an **ENDANGERED** amphibian found only in eastern Texas.
- While they are called the Houston toad, there are no longer any living in the wild in Houston.

HOUSTON TOAD

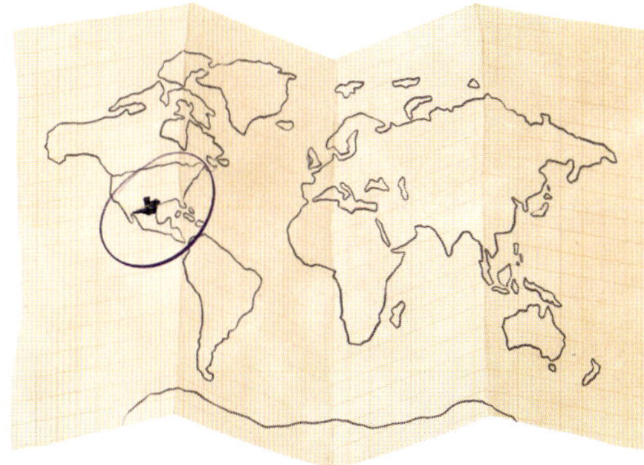

The Houston toad is only found in eastern Texas. They are *habitat specialists*, which means they need to live in a very specific habitat to survive. They need deep sand so they can burrow for protection when it is hot and dry, and shallow ponds for breeding. They prefer forests with post oak trees or loblolly pine trees that thrive in sandy soil and give plenty of canopy coverage.

The female Houston toad can lay two thousand to six thousand eggs at a time! The eggs are strung together like a strand of beads. The tadpoles hatch and live in the pond between two-and-a-half and seven weeks. Then, as small toads, they live on land near the water for a few more weeks before venturing into the forest.

Human construction and wildfires have destroyed much of the Houston toads' natural habitat. The toads are also in danger from pollution, roads, and invasive species. Even pets, like dogs and cats, are a threat.

ANIMAL VOICE

Males have a bright blue throat sac that fills up with air when they call. Their call is a high-pitched trill, which can last between twenty and thirty seconds at a time.

WHAT ARE WE DOING?

Government and private organizations, as well as zoos, have come together to help protect this species. Restoring and managing habitats is very important to their survival. Zoos are breeding Houston toads and releasing eggs and young toads into the wild.

QUICK FACTS

- The white-backed vulture is an **ENDANGERED** bird found in sub-Saharan Africa.
- To cool off in hot weather, white-backed vultures will pee on their feet and legs. The urine kills bugs and germs, which helps keep the vulture healthy.

WHITE-BACKED VULTURE

Vultures sometimes have a bad reputation, but they play an important role in keeping their ecosystem healthy by working as a clean-up crew. They eat only *carrion*, which is a fancy word for dead animals. Getting rid of meat before it can rot prevents dangerous germs from growing.. Vultures also act as insect control because some insect populations become too large if there is a lot of rot for them to eat.

The white-backed vulture is spread throughout sub-Saharan Africa. Their wingspan can reach seven feet wide! They hunt for carrion by circling in the sky with keen eyesight. These social animals eat together, sometimes with as many as one hundred vultures joining the meal. Sometimes they eat so much, they cannot fly afterward!

They roost together in tall trees and breed once a year. They lay only one egg, and the parents take turns caring for it for about two months. Once it hatches, the chick stays in the nest for about four months before it is ready to fly.

One of the biggest dangers to white-backed vultures is poisoning from the food they eat. Vultures sometimes eat poisoned meat left out by farmers to kill the animals they believe will harm their livestock; cattle that have been given medicine to keep them healthy; and bullets left in animals that have been shot. These vultures are also used in traditional medicine.

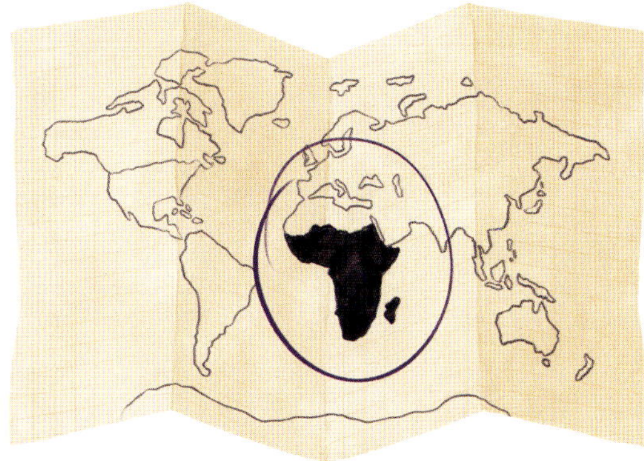

ANIMAL VOICE

The white-backed vulture is silent most of the time, but it occasionally sounds like a pig, making chittering and squealing noises.

WHAT ARE WE DOING?

Conservation organizations monitor the locations where vultures are getting poisoned and work to stop poachers. They also help build systems around cattle to prevent predators from getting to them, which would then attract the vultures.

The Association of Zoos and Aquariums has a program called Saving Animals From Extinction (SAFE). The white-backed vulture is one of the animals they help by educating the public about the animal and its importance, as well as breeding and helping sick or injured vultures for release back into the wild.

QUICK FACTS

- The blue whale is an **ENDANGERED** mammal found in every ocean of the world except the Arctic Ocean.
- We can learn how old a blue whale is by counting the layers in its earwax.

BLUE WHALE

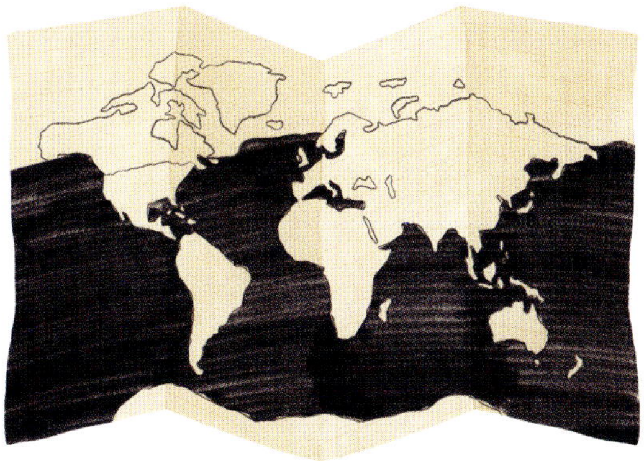

The largest animal ever known to exist on the planet, the blue whale is about seventy to ninety feet long, which is as long as three school buses. They can weigh between 200,000 and 300,000 pounds, which is as heavy as eight school buses!

This giant creature feeds mostly on krill, which are tiny, shrimp-like creatures that swim in swarms. Krill are the main food source for hundreds of animals. Blue whales can eat about eight thousand pounds of krill each day! Instead of teeth, blue whales have flexible plates that act like combs, called baleen. Sucking large amounts of water and krill into their mouths, the whales then push the water out with their tongues and the krill are caught in the baleen.

Females give birth every two to three years. A newborn calf measures about twenty-three feet long and already weighs up to six thousand pounds! It drinks its mother's milk and can gain up to two hundred and fifty pounds per day for the first few months of its life.

Blue whales used to be hunted for their fat (called blubber), which was used in soaps and oil lamps, and for the flexible baleen, which was used in fashion to make hoop skirts, corsets, and hats. In 1966, the International Whaling Commission banned the hunting of blue whales.

ANIMAL VOICE

Blue whales are one of the loudest animals on Earth. Because these solitary animals are spread out across the oceans, they need this volume to communicate over long distances. In good conditions, their calls can travel one thousand miles! Blue whales make sounds that humans can hear—such as grunts, hums, moans, and clicks—but they can also make sounds too low for humans to hear.

WHAT ARE WE DOING?

The biggest threats to the blue whales are climate change, human fishing and shipping, and polluted waters. Scientists track and follow these giants using satellite tags to see where they live and which routes they use to migrate. Conservationists and governments work together to protect these areas and redirect shipping lanes to avoid human-whale conflict.

QUICK FACTS

- The grey-headed flying fox is a **VULNERABLE** mammal found in Australia.
- During extreme heat, the flying fox will fly to lakes or rivers and skim the surface of the water, getting their bellies wet, to cool themselves.

GREY-HEADED FLYING FOX

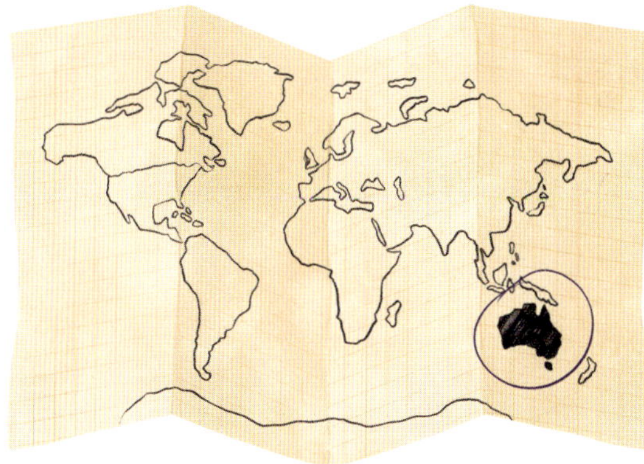

With a wingspan of three feet, one of the largest bats in Australia is the grey-headed flying fox. They are the only flying fox species with a collar of orange-brown fur that wraps around their head. Much like butterflies and honeybees, the grey-headed flying fox is an important pollinator.

Their diet consists of fruit and nectar. While they eat, their furry faces collect pollen and transfer it to other flowers. They also spread fruit seeds as they eat. Individuals travel an average of thirty miles each night in search of food!

A group of flying foxes is known as a camp and can be made up of thousands of flying foxes. The young are carried by their mothers for the first three weeks of their lives, even while they fly. Once they are too heavy to carry, all the babies of the camp are left in a crèche, or nursery, while the mothers look for food. Even when mothers return to large groups of babies, they can find their baby by its scent. The young learn to fly when they are about three months old.

ANIMAL VOICE

Grey-headed flying foxes do not use echolocation like some bats. Instead, these talkative creatures can make more than thirty specific calls! Their most common calls are squeals, shrieks, and cackles.

WHAT ARE WE DOING?

The biggest cause of their decline is the loss of their forest habitat. As a result, they travel further and to new locations to find food, which leads them to orchards. Farmers then kill these "pests" who are eating their crops.

Australia is working hard to protect the grey-headed flying fox by stabilizing the population, protecting essential habitat, and developing nonharmful control methods in problem areas, such as orchards.

QUICK FACTS

- The black rhino is a **CRITICALLY ENDANGERED** mammal found in Africa.
- Black rhinos are not black; they are gray. We do not really know where they got their name! It may be from the dark-colored soil that covers its skin after wallowing in mud, to separate them from the white rhino, or as a translation from "beak," which describes their lip shape.

BLACK RHINO

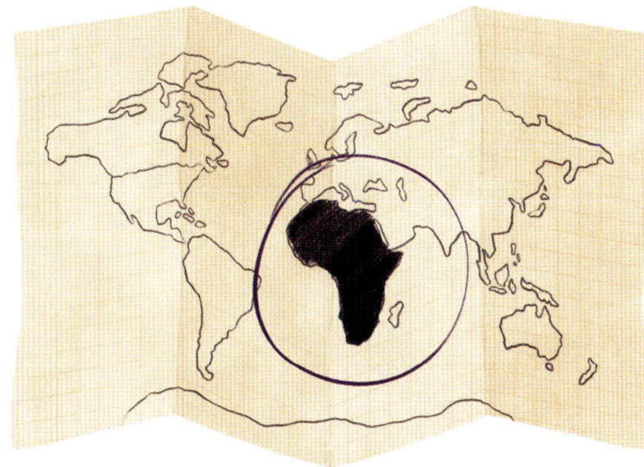

There are two species of rhinoceros, or rhino, in Africa. The larger is the white rhino, and the smaller is the black rhino. One big difference between the two species is the shape of their mouths. The white rhino's mouth is square-shaped for eating grasses, while the black rhino's is pointy, like a beak, which helps it eat leaves and branches from trees and bushes.

Most black rhinos stand just over five feet tall and weigh between 1,760 and 3,080 pounds. They have an excellent sense of smell and hearing, but their eyesight is not very good. Their skin may be thick, but it is sensitive. To protect their skin from the sun and bugs, they relax in water holes and mud. Their horns are made of keratin, which is what human hair and fingernails are made of.

They live mostly solitary lives. Only females and their young travel together. A female may give birth every two to three years, and a calf stays with its mother for about two years before going off on its own. Rhinos can be aggressive and territorial. They have even been seen charging at trains moving through their territory.

ANIMAL VOICE

Rhinos make many sounds, including sniffing, grunting, growling, mooing, panting, squealing, screaming, and trumpeting. The high-pitched squeals are mostly made by the calves.

WHAT ARE WE DOING?

The biggest threat to the black rhino is poaching. Their horns are used in traditional medicine, and with two horns, they are seen as more valuable to the poachers.

Conservation groups and local governments are working together to protect the black rhino's habitat. They work with local people and use technology to catch and stop poachers from harming these protected animals.

QUICK FACTS

- The Philippine eagle is a **CRITICALLY ENDANGERED** bird found in the forests of the Philippines.
- Their wingspan can reach seven feet wide, and a mane-like crest surrounds their head.

PHILIPPINE EAGLE

The Philippine eagle is a rare bird found only on four islands in the Philippines—Luzon, Samar, Leyte, and Mindanao. They live in dense forests hunting birds, snakes, and small mammals like monkeys and civets.

They launch themselves straight up for takeoff, and, even with a large wingspan, they can travel easily through branches and vines. Sometimes the eagles work together to hunt; one eagle distracts their prey while the other attacks from behind.

Both the mother and father care for the young. Females lay only one egg every two years. The parents take turns warming the egg, hunting, and feeding the chick. The chick grows quickly but will not take its first flight until it is about five months old.

Humans are the main threat to the Philippine eagle. Loggers and farmers clear land where the eagle lives, hunters kill them as prizes, and farmers spray pesticides that harm them and their eggs.

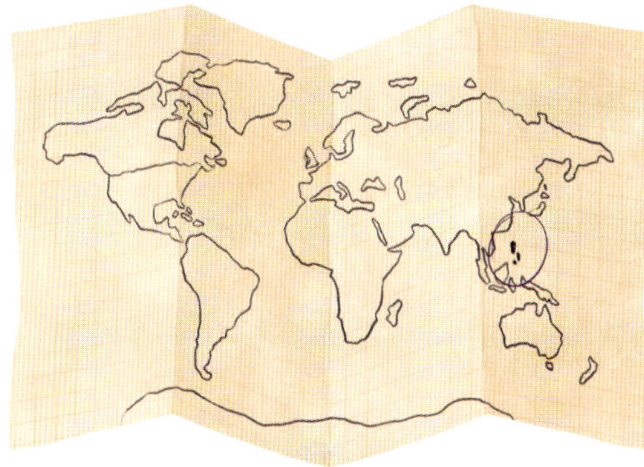

ANIMAL VOICE

The long, high-pitched calls and the short shrieks of the Philippine eagle carry through the forests. Philippine eagles make various calls and whistles while hunting or communicating with their family. Caretakers of Philippine eagles in captivity whistle and mimic the bird's vocalizations when working with the birds to help calm them during feeding, bonding activities, and educational demonstrations.

WHAT ARE WE DOING?

The Philippine Eagle Foundation works with local communities to track, monitor, and protect the eagles and their nests. They also educate the public about the importance of the Philippines' national bird. Breeding programs have also been put in place. Most importantly, multiple organizations are working to protect and conserve the forests the eagles live in.

QUICK FACTS

- The Bengal tiger is an **ENDANGERED** mammal found in India, Bangladesh, Nepal, and Bhutan.
- Tigers have webbed toes and are excellent swimmers.

BENGAL TIGER

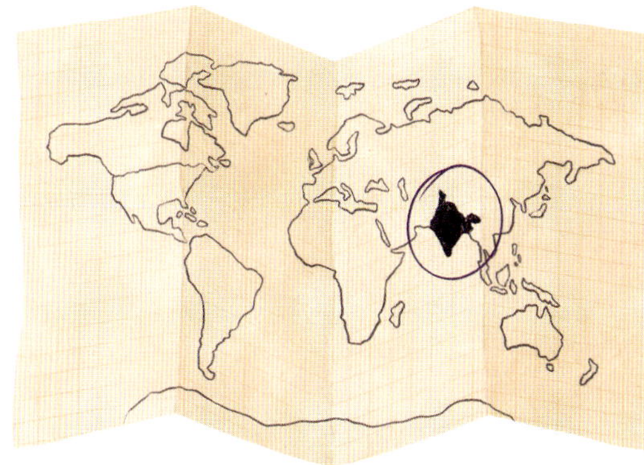

Bengal tigers, sometimes called Indian tigers, make up half of the world's population of tigers. Tigers are the largest of the big cats. Bengal tigers weigh between three hundred and five hundred pounds and are between five to six feet long. Their tails add another two to three feet to their length. No two tigers have the same stripe pattern.

In the wild, a tiger's life span averages fifteen years, but Bengal tigers have been recorded to have lived up to twenty-six years old in captivity! Living solitary lives, they mark their territories with their scent to ward off intruders. They have canine teeth that are almost four inches long and soft pads on their feet that help them move silently. Bengal tigers hunt primarily at dusk and dawn. Using their striped camouflage, they stalk their prey, which includes deer and wild pigs. They can eat up to eighty-eight pounds at once, although they usually eat less.

A litter of babies has two to six cubs that are raised by their mother alone. At about eighteen months old, the cubs start to hunt. They'll stay with their mother for two to three years before setting off to find territories of their own.

ANIMAL VOICE

Bengal tigers make a variety of sounds including growls, roars, snarls, and prustens, also known as chuffs. A chuff is made when they keep their mouth closed and push air out of their nose. Their roar can be heard up to two miles away! Researchers have even recorded their sounds and discovered they can identify individuals in the wild and track them.

WHAT ARE WE DOING?

The wild Bengal tiger population has greatly declined. They have lost most of their habitat due to human activities, and they are poached for their distinct coats and use in traditional medicine.

Conservation groups work at protecting national parks, reintroducing tigers to the wild, preventing poaching, and reducing human-tiger conflict. Some groups have come together to preserve millions of acres of land to secure the future of these great cats.

BIBLIOGRAPHY

"What Does 'Endangered Species' Mean?" WWF. World Wildlife Fund. http://www.worldwildlife.org/pages/what-does-endangered-species-mean.

"The IUCN Red List of Threatened Species." IUCN Red List of Threatened Species. https://www.iucnredlist.org/.

1. BLACK-FOOTED FERRET

"Black-Footed Ferret Facts: The Masked Bandits of the Northern Great Plains." WWF. World Wildlife Fund, May 12, 2014. https://www.worldwildlife.org/stories/black-footed-ferret-facts-the-masked-bandits-of-the-northern-great-plains.

"Black Footed Ferret." YouTube. Arizona Game And Fish, April 30, 2007. https://www.youtube.com/watch?v=TrwMjThKQ_g.

"Black-Footed Ferret." Smithsonian's National Zoo, October 3, 2019. https://nationalzoo.si.edu/animals/black-footed-ferret.

Earth Rangers. "Black-Footed Ferret and Conservation." YouTube. Earth Rangers, November 23, 2011. https://www.youtube.com/watch?v=ta-mukf5Ucw.

2. KĀKĀPŌ

Arakawa , Kristin. "Happy Hatchday: 21 Years of Conservation Success for the Kākāpō." National Geographic Society Newsroom, March 23, 2018. https://blog.nationalgeographic.org/2018/03/22/happy-hatchday-21-years-of-conservation-success-for-the-kākāpō/.

Gerard Hutching, 'Large forest birds - Kākāpō', Te Ara - the Encyclopedia of New Zealand, http://www.TeAra.govt.nz/en/video/10577/male-kākāpō-booming.

Gray, Claudia. "Kākāpō on the EDGE: the Fight to Save the World's Weirdest Parrot." EDGE of Existence, January 19, 2018. https://www.edgeofexistence.org/blog/kākāpō-edge-fight-save-worlds-weirdest-parrot/.

"How New Zealand's Rare Kākāpō Is Making a Comeback - CNN Video." CNN. Cable News Network, December 26, 2019. https://www.cnn.com/videos/world/2019/12/20/kākāpō-new-zealand-c2e.cnn/video/playlists/call-to-earth/.

"Kākāpō Coprolite Yields Conservation Clues." Science, January 22, 2013. https://www.nationalgeographic.com/science/phenomena/2013/01/22/kākāpō-coprolite-yields-conservation-clues/.

"Kākāpō Recovery." Department of Conservation. Accessed January 5, 2021. https://www.doc.govt.nz/our-work/kākāpō-recovery/.

"The New Zealand Kākāpō - The World's Most Endangered Bird." Go to New Zealand, July 25, 2019. https://www.gotonewzealand.co.nz/kākāpō/.

3. SUMATRAN ORANGUTAN

Ferguson, PhD, Stephen M. "Photo Ark: Sumatran Orangutan." National Geographic Society, December 20, 2018. https://www.nationalgeographic.org/media/photo-ark-sumatran-orangutan/.

Home - SOCP. https://www.sumatranorangutan.org/sumatran-orangutans/.

National Geographic Society. "Sumatran Wonders." National Geographic Society, December 17, 2020. https://www.nationalgeographic.org/video/wildindonesia_episode2_25i_clip1/.

"Sumatran Orangutan." Denver Zoo. https://denverzoo.org/animals/sumatran-orangutan/.

"Sumatran Orangutan." WWF. World Wildlife Fund. https://www.worldwildlife.org/species/sumatran-orangutan.

4. POLAR BEAR

"Climate Change." Polar Bears and Climate Change - Polar Bears International. https://polarbearsinternational.org/climate-change.

Feltman, Rachel. "Why Do Polar Bears Look so White?" The Washington Post. WP Company, December 17, 2017. https://www.washingtonpost.com/lifestyle/kidspost/why-do-polar-bears-look-so-white/2017/12/15/6a8301f4-d5ee-11e7-95bf-df7c19270879_story.html.

"Polar Bear." Lincoln Park Zoo, August 20, 2020. https://www.lpzoo.org/animal/polar-bear.

"Polar Bear Reproduction." Polar Bear Reproduction | WWF Arctic. Accessed January 5, 2021. https://arcticwwf.org/species/polar-bear/reproduction/.

polarbearsinternat. "Polar Bear Sounds." YouTube. Polar Bears International, November 7, 2010. https://www.youtube.com/watch?v=0k60A6nflNA.

Sartore, Joel - photographer. "Polar Bear: National Geographic." National Geographic, September 21, 2018. https://www.nationalgeographic.com/animals/mammals/p/polar-bear/.

5. COTTON-TOP TAMARIN

"Cotton-Top Tamarin." National Geographic, April 1, 2020. https://www.nationalgeographic.com/animals/mammals/c/cotton-top-tamarin/.

"Cotton-Top Tamarin." New England Primate Conservancy. Accessed January 5, 2021. https://www.neprimateconservancy.org/cotton-top-tamarin.html.

"Cotton-Top Tamarins." Proyecto Tití: Conserving the Cotton-top Tamarin in Colombia > Home. Accessed January 5, 2021. https://www.proyectotiti.com/en-us/Cotton-top-Tamarins/Cotton-Top-Tamarins.

"Cotton-Top Tamarin." Oakland Zoo. Accessed January 5, 2021. https://www.oaklandzoo.org/animals/cotton-top-tamarin.

6. RED WOLF

"All About the Red Wolf." National Geographic, July 26, 2019. https://www.nationalgeographic.com/animals/mammals/r/red-wolf/.

nywolforg. "Red Wolf Pack Howling." YouTube. Wolf Conservation Center, February 18, 2011. https://www.youtube.com/watch?v=QUK2z6bynlg.

"Red Wolf." National Wildlife Federation. https://www.nwf.org/Educational-Resources/Wildlife-Guide/Mammals/Red-Wolf.

"Red Wolf." U.S. Fish & Wildlife Service. https://www.fws.gov/southeast/wildlife/mammals/red-wolf/.

7. ASIAN ELEPHANT

"Asian Elephant." Encyclopedia Britannica. Encyclopedia Britannica, Inc. https://www.britannica.com/animal/Asian-elephant.

"Asian Elephant: National Geographic." National Geographic, July 5, 2019. https://www.nationalgeographic.com/animals/mammals/a/asian-elephant/.

"Asian Elephant." WWF. World Wildlife Fund. https://www.worldwildlife.org/species/asian-elephant.

Sharma, Nachiketha, Vijay Prakash S, Shiro Kohshima, and Raman Sukumar. "Asian Elephants Modulate Their Vocalizations When Disturbed." Animal Behaviour. Academic Press, January 15, 2020. https://www.sciencedirect.com/science/article/abs/pii/S0003347219303938.

8. HOUSTON TOAD

"Can We Save These Rare Toads From Extinction? | National Geographic." YouTube. National Geographic, November 12, 2015. https://www.youtube.com/watch?v=RHVIymD3Ppk.

The Houston Toad. http://thehoustontoad.org/?page_id=21.

National Geographic Society. "Houston Toad." National Geographic Society. Accessed January 5, 2021. http://www.nationalgeographic.org/projects/photo-ark/animal/anaxyrus-houstonensis/.

U.S. Fish and Wildlife Service. "Houston Toad - Ecological Services, Southwest Region Fish and Wildlife Service." Official Web page of the U S Fish and Wildlife Service. https://www.fws.gov/ifw2es/HoustonToad/.

9. WHITE-BACKED VULTURE

"African White-Backed Vulture." African White-backed Vulture | The Peregrine Fund. https://peregrinefund.org/explore-raptors-species/vultures/african-white-backed-vulture.

BirdLife International (2021) Species factsheet: Gyps africanus. Downloaded from http://www.birdlife.org

"White-Backed Vulture." National Geographic, March 24, 2020. https://www.nationalgeographic.com/animals/birds/w/white-backed-vulture/.

PAC2013. "White-Backed Vulture (Gyps Africanus)." The Mohamed bin Zayed Species Conservation Fund. Accessed January 5, 2021. https://www.speciesconservation.org/case-studies-projects/white-backed-vulture/11037.

10. BLUE WHALE

Blue Whale: Baleen Whales: Voices in the Sea. http://cetus.ucsd.edu/voicesinthesea_org/species/baleenWhales/blue.html.

"Blue Whale." National Geographic, June 9, 2020. https://www.nationalgeographic.com/animals/mammals/b/blue-whale/.

"Blue Whales' Food Supply Under Threat in the Antarctic." WWF. World Wildlife Fund, July 19, 2001. https://www.worldwildlife.org/press-releases/blue-whales-food-supply-under-threat-in-the-antarctic.

"Blue Whale." The Marine Mammal Center. https://www.marinemammalcenter.org/animal-care/learn-about-marine-mammals/cetaceans/blue-whale.

"National Geographic: Disney Australia & New Zealand." Disney Australia, July 19, 1970. https://www.nationalgeographic.com.au/science/blue-whales-and-communication.aspx.

"Sounds of the Blue Whale - California." YouTube. NatGeoOceans, January 8, 2009. https://www.youtube.com/watch?v=i8MTsgdWuU0.

11. GREY-HEADED FLYING FOX

"Back from the Brink - Season 2 Episode 2 - Grey-Headed Flying-Fox." YouTube. Natura Pacific, June 2, 2019. https://www.youtube.com/watch?v=2xhrAg4TzMo.

Gimesy, Doug-Photographer. "Meet Australia's Urban Flying Foxes-and the People Trying to Help Them." National Geographic, January 7, 2020. https://www.nationalgeographic.com/animals/2018/11/flying-foxes-bats-animal-rescue-australia/.

"Grey-Headed Flying-Fox." The Australian Museum. https://australianmuseum.net.au/learn/animals/bats/grey-headed-flying-fox/.

"Grey-Headed Flying-Fox." Wildlife Preservation Society Queensland - WPSQ. https://wildlife.org.au/grey-headed-flying-fox/.

National Geographic Society. "Vulnerable Grey-Headed Flying Fox." National Geographic Society. https://www.nationalgeographic.org/projects/photo-ark/animal/pteropus-poliocephalus/.

12. BLACK RHINO

"Black Rhinoceros: National Geographic." National Geographic, September 21, 2018. https://www.nationalgeographic.com/animals/mammals/b/black-rhinoceros/.

"Black Rhino: Species: Save the Rhino International." Save The Rhino. Accessed January 6, 2021. https://www.savetherhino.org/rhino-info/rhino-species/black-rhinos/.

"Black Rhino." WWF. World Wildlife Fund. https://www.worldwildlife.org/species/black-rhino.

DiLonardo, Mary Jo. "What's the Difference Between Black Rhinos and White Rhinos?" Treehugger. https://www.treehugger.com/difference-between-black-rhinos-and-white-rhinos-4864405.

"What Sound Does a Rhino Make? Learn It All!" Africa Freak, March 8, 2019. https://africafreak.com/what-sound-does-a-rhino-make.

13. PHILIPPINE EAGLE

Danan, Tammy, and August 24. "A Noble Eagle on the Edge of Extinction Thrives Under Devoted Caretakers." Audubon, August 28, 2018. https://www.audubon.org/news/a-noble-eagle-edge-extinction-thrives-under-devoted-caretakers.

Liner, Eric, director. Rettig, Neil, cinematographer. 20179. Bird of Prey. The Cornell Lab of Ornithology.

NatGeoWild. "Watch an Endangered Philippine Eagle Chick Grow Up in Rare Video | Nat Geo Wild." YouTube. Nat Geo Wild, February 5, 2019. https://www.youtube.com/watch?v=-JP-zoBLyWE.

"Philippine Eagle." Philippine Eagle | The Peregrine Fund. https://peregrinefund.org/explore-raptors-species/eagles/philippine-eagle.

"The Philippine Eagle." Philippine Eagle Foundation. https://www.philippineeaglefoundation.org/the-philippine-eagle.

14. BENGAL TIGER

"Decoding a Tiger's Chuffs, Roars, and Groans." Sierra Club, June 28, 2017. https://www.sierraclub.org/sierra/decoding-tigers-chuffs-roars-and-groans.

Society, National Geographic. "Tigers." National Geographic Society. https://www.nationalgeographic.org/topics/tigers/.

Sartore, Joel, photographer. "Bengal Tiger: National Geographic." National Geographic, December 31, 2020. https://www.nationalgeographic.com/animals/mammals/b/bengal-tiger/.

"Tiger." WWF. World Wildlife Fund. https://www.worldwildlife.org/species/tiger.

ABOUT THE AUTHOR

JUNE SMALLS

June Smalls is the author of *She Leads: The Elephant Matriarch* and *He Leads: Mountain Gorilla, the Gentle Giant*. She is a member of the Society of Children's Book Writers and Illustrators and a lover of literature. She resides in Northern Virginia with her hubby, The Kid, and an ever-growing assortment of animals.

ABOUT THE ILLUSTRATOR

BECKY THORNS

Becky Thorns is an illustrator and lettering artist based in Cornwall, United Kingdom, whose detailed and textured illustration style focus on narrative and adventure. When Becky is not working, you can find her exploring the great outdoors or inside, cozy with a documentary, usually true crime or wildlife.

ABOUT FAMILIUS

Familius is a global trade publishing company that publishes books and other content to help families be happy. We believe that the family is the fundamental unit of society and that happy families are the foundation of a happy life. We recognize that every family looks different, and we passionately believe in helping all families find greater joy. To that end, we publish books for children and adults that invite families to live the Familius Ten Habits of Happy Families: *love together, play together, learn together, work together, talk together, heal together, read together, eat together, give together,* and *laugh together*. Founded in 2012, Familius is located in Sanger, California.

Website: www.familius.com
Facebook: www.facebook.com/familiustalk
Twitter: @familiustalk, @paterfamilius1
Pinterest: www.pinterest.com/familius
Instagram: @familiustalk

FAMILIUS

Published by Familius LLC, www.familius.com

PO Box 1249, Reedley, CA 93654

Familius books are available at special discounts for bulk purchases, whether for sales promotions or for family or corporate use. For more information, contact Familius Sales at orders@familius.com.

Library of Congress Control Number: 2022939970

Print ISBN 978-1-64170-728-2

Printed in China

Edited by Peg Sandkam and Erin R. Lund

Cover design by Carlos Guerrero

Book design by Brooke Jorden

10 9 8 7 6 5 4 3 2 1

First Edition